About the Author

Having introduced over ten thousand people to dowsing, over the last three decades Dean has become one of the world's leading advocates of dowsing as a means of connecting to our own intuition, also a passionate teacher of meditation and holistic lifestyles. His Unlock Your Life books on Dowsing have become a worldwide phenomenon ranked in the top-selling on hundred genre titles year in year out on Amazon.

"To me dowsing is all about learning to trust our intuition. Once we are more attuned to our intuition, life takes on a whole new meaning and will become fascinating in ways you might never have before conceived" - Dean Fraser.

www.deanfrasercentral.com

Books and Audios by Dean Fraser

UNLOCK YOUR LIFE WITH PENDULUM DOWSING BOOKS
Book One - Anyone Can Dowse
Book Two - Spiritual Healing
Book Three - Crystals In Your Life
Book Four – You Were Born To Dowse

AUDIO BOOKS
Pendulum Dowsing & Crystal Healing
Pendulum Dowsing & Spiritual Healing
Unlock Your Life With Pendulum Dowsing

ALSO
Dowsing Ghosts & Psychic Healing Casebook

Books are available from www.deanfrasercentral.com and all good online bookstores

Unlock Your Life With
Pendulum Dowsing

Book Four

You Were Born To Dowse

Dean Fraser

First published in 2021

Copyright © Dean Fraser 2021

Dean Fraser has asserted his right under the Copyright, Designs and Patents Act 1988 to be identified as the author of this book and work.

ISBN 9798704656081

Although the author and publisher have made every effort to ensure that the information in this book was correct at press time, the author and publisher do not assume and hereby disclaim any liability to any party for any loss, damage, or disruption caused by errors or omissions, whether such errors or omissions result from negligence, accident, or any other cause. This book is not intended as a substitute for the medical advice of medical professionals. The reader should regularly consult a chosen medical professional in matters relating to his/her health and particularly with respect to any symptoms that may require diagnosis or medical attention.

For all the people, past, present and future (now) who have
inspired and helped me. You know who you are!

Contents

Foreword   08

Introduction - A Brief History of Dowsing   10

Rod Or Pendulum Dowsing?   14

Pure Dowsing   16

Life Choices   21

Developing as a Dowser   25

Dowsing Lists   29

Ley Lines and Investigating the Landscape   32

What Do You Think?   41

Dowsing And Meditation   47

Signs to Take Action   50

Water   52

Finding Lost Objects   57

Cleansing Your Pendulum   60

Putting It All Together   61

Foreword

I intend for this book to be a follow-up to the first Unlock Your Life With Pendulum Dowsing book in the series, namely Anyone Can Dowse. Whilst that book was written to act as an introduction to dowsing, You Were Born To Dowse takes the premise rather further, and although for those new to dowsing there is a chapter entitled Pure Dowsing detailing exactly how to dowse, the overall essence of this book is to stretch my reader's dowsing to help them gain insights in all areas of their lives.

As I will reiterate several times during the following pages, I see dowsing as an incredibly efficient way for developing and nurturing trust in our own intuition.

Once we learn to trust our intuition, life will take on a whole new meaning and will for sure get interesting in ways you will have to discover for yourself!

I indeed followed my own intuition upon waking one morning with the overriding need to pen this fourth addition to my series of Unlock Your Life With Pendulum Dowsing books. May you also have similar moments of inspiration and insight, and above all enjoy this book as much as I enjoyed writing it for you.

Dean Fraser
2021

www.deanfrasercentral.com

Introduction - A Brief History of Dowsing

Nobody is quite sure when dowsing first came into being. Cave paintings suggest people were dowsing back into pre-history. Our ancient ancestors undoubtedly knew how to read the land and place their sacred sites in alignment with the Earth's natural energy grid, or Ley Lines. Could it be these priests and shamans were dowsers?

It seems entirely likely, although obviously no written records remain to confirm this. How else could they have been so accurate in their calculations? Dowsers today confirming these ancients knew exactly where to place their temples, burial grounds and ceremonial sites within the landscape to ensure alignment with Ley Lines.

Back in 1691 Somerset born philosopher John Locke coined the phrase "deusing-rods". In an essay Locke wrote of mineral and water exploration; it is generally believed he took the phrase from the ancient Gaelic Cornish language where "dewsys" meant goddess and "rhod" meant tree branch.

There had been literary references to dowsing before this, however, Locke was the first to coin the phrase dowsing in relation to divining with rods or hazel twig.

It is possible that rod dowsing was introduced into Cornwall from Germany through the mining industry. There is a famous woodcutting showing a twig dowser walking around a mining site in a 1550's edition of German cartographer Sebastian Munter's, Cosmographia.

German mining engineers were in great demand, regularly travelling to other countries to lend their expertise. With its vast mineral wealth Cornwall would have been one such place, and it is entirely likely they taught dowsing for minerals to local miners. It is known that German miners were using dowsing in Welsh silver mines in the 17th century.

Although twig or rod dowsing can be traced down through history, often through their usefulness in locating water or ore, the use of pendulums is a little trickier to locate back through the mists of time. Perhaps pendulums were used more for personal dowsing, rather than exploring the landscape, and as such escaped the attention of artists and scholars?

Pendulum dowsing certainly grew in popularity during the 19th century and continues to attract more adherents with each passing decade.

Dowsing is still used for finding minerals and ore today.

Rod Or Pendulum Dowsing?

Pendulums work in situations where rods or twig would be difficult or impossible to apply. They are especially useful within the fields of dowsing lists, psychic development, map dowsing, spiritual healing and testing food. Most of these applications would become unnecessarily complicated with applying rods or twigs; a pendulum however is ideal.

Pendulums are also usefully portable, they easily fit into a pocket or small bag. Taken out to use as required and then easily stowed away again until next time. They are also discreet, avoiding the interested attention the rod or twig dowser usually attracts.

When landscape dowsing, if the weather is inclement, we can use our pendulum to dowse maps from the comfort of our car or indeed even our favourite armchair.

Another advantage of opting for a pendulum becomes clear when asking questions from dowsing. We get an extremely specific and consistent response from a pendulum. The skill can sometimes be in later interpreting these results within the context of our lives. We will deal more with learning to trust intuition as we progress on our dowsing journey together.

Which style of pendulum to go for is a purely personal choice. There are myriads of options available from metals such as brass or copper, then crystal or semi-precious gemstones, and through to a variety different natural wood options. And finally we can even craft a pendulum for ourselves using a plumb bob on a piece of cord or choose a heavy old-style door key, again suspended on a cord. As long as the weight hangs straight and true, we have a practical pendulum.

Pure Dowsing

You want to ensure your dowsing will be pure and real from day one. This exercise will guarantee this is the case.

A pendulum works by responding in movements to specific questions asked of it. These movements will be in one of three different ways. The given answer will always be YES, NO or MAYBE.

So every time we ask any kind of question our pendulum will move in one of these three ways and we arrive at our answer. The specific direction a pendulum moves in answer to a question varies from person to person. There is no right or wrong here. Movements can include clockwise or counter-clockwise rotation, forward and backward swinging, side to side swinging, diagonal swinging or even ovoid rotation.

You can establish your own dowsing pendulum responses through this exercise.

Take a piece of card and evenly spaced write YES, NO and MAYBE on it, then cut them out to make three identical sized squares of card.

Find somewhere quiet to sit where there is no chance of you being disturbed. A place far away from everyday distractions such as children, partners, televisions, radios, computers, phones or indeed any of the other thousand and one things that could spoil your concentration. You are going to establish what are your personal pendulum movements when asking any question.

Take the pendulum in your projective hand, which is the one you usually write with. Hold it by pinching the chain or cord between your thumb and forefinger, allowing about 15cm (6 inches) to hang freely before reaching the pendulum (you don't need to measure this, just approximately will be fine!), wrap any remaining length of cord inside your hand.

Holding your pendulum over the piece of card with YES written on it. Say out loud or in your head, while focusing on the writing "what is my YES response?"

Be patient as this can take a few seconds to get a response to start off with. Then the pendulum will start to slowly vibrate and then gently at first move in a specific direction.

Let it move in this direction for at least a minute once it is freely swinging. This can seem a little eerie at first, watching the pendulum swinging of its own accord. From now on this direction will now always be your YES answer to any question you may ask your pendulum.

Having firmly established your YES response, logically you can now move on to NO next. Hold your pendulum over the piece of card with NO written on it. Ask the question out loud or in your head "what is my NO response?" and slowly the pendulum will take on a movement in a definite direction, but different from your YES direction.

Once again let it swing freely for at least a minute. You have now also your established NO response to any question you may ask of your pendulum.

At this point, by using your pendulum to ask questions you will be able to establish a definite YES or NO response.

MAYBE comes into play if a question you ask does not have a readily available or obvious YES or NO response answer.

A MAYBE response enables us to ask the question again in another way for a definite YES or NO response. Or wait until some later date or time to have another go. Then again we sometimes have to accept that there are simply some things we are not yet meant to know. This can often happen when using a pendulum for attempting the prediction of future outcomes of events in life - as there are often so many unforeseen variables which can come into play, a specific YES or NO is impossible.

Take the card with MAYBE written on it. Naturally, this works exactly the same as with when you established your YES and NO responses. Hold your pendulum over the MAYBE card and ask out loud or to yourself "what is my MAYBE response?" Once more your pendulum will take on a movement, different from your YES and NO.

Let it carry on swinging for at least a minute to be sure of your directional movement and from this moment this will then always be your MAYBE response.

Once you have completed these exercises you will have all you need to get started with dowsing. You have your YES, NO or MAYBE response to any question you care to ask and your pendulum will always give you one of those three answers.

As we will learn, the art is in phrasing the questions to get the best possible use out of our pendulum. A good rule to remember is that pendulums will always work in a rather literal way; it is up to us to interpret the answers we get within the context of our own lives and what they mean to us.

Life Choices

Claire found herself faced with a life changing decision. She loved James and he had asked her to marry him. Therein lay her issue. Claire was used to living on her own in her small flat, she enjoyed the freedom of choice on what and when to eat, which colour to paint the walls, she enjoyed reading for hours when she felt like it and then there was her slightly obsessive sense of organising her stuff exactly how she liked it within her personal space.

She hadn't lived with anyone since her house-sharing student days over a decade before; and James wished them to both sell their flats and buy a house to begin their married life together.

On the one hand Claire loved the idea of sharing her life with her soul mate, then again the way such a radical change in her lifestyle would make her feel couldn't be ignored.

As a recent dowser, Claire took her pendulum to ask the question "should I marry James?" To receive a definite NO response.

Shocked at her dowsing response, and more than a little upset at the prospect of losing James, Claire decided to write down all her reasons for and against marriage.

Her "for marriage" list included sharing her life with the someone she loved beyond all doubt, at some point having children with James, loving and feeling loved.

Her "against marriage" list mainly centred on losing her freedom of choice.

Looking at her two lists for a little while made Claire see exactly why her dowsing responses had been consistently NO when she asked if she should marry. Her subconscious fears had prejudiced her dowsing responses.

Remaining impartial can be one of the greatest challenges when using a dowsing pendulum to answer more personal questions. It can be all too easy to influence the responses we get through our subconscious fears and misgivings.

If you are dowsing seeking answers to more personal questions and seem to be getting an illogical response from your pendulum, one which either sees you staying right where you are doing what you have always done or alternatively if a YES response doesn't seem to sit quite right with you; then it is time to write a list.

Like Claire did, write down how the situation makes you feel, take time to do this so you can get the heart of any latent issues you might have buried deep in your subconscious mind.

Once Claire realised her feared loss of freedom all came not really from the thought of getting married, but rather moving out of her safe-space into somewhere brand new; she saw the situation more in context. She came to see this first house together with James as offering her far more freedom that her current life offered, here they could build a beautiful new home together and she loved the thought of making it personal to both of their tastes.

Dowsing again a week later, asking the question should she get married, gave Claire a resounding YES response from her pendulum.

Dowsing will always get right to the heart of a matter, even if it is only revealing any underlying subconscious feelings we may have which are hindering our dowsing responses, allowing us the opportunity to deal with them and move forward.

Developing as a Dowser

As we have just established, one of the greatest challenges in dowsing is overcoming our own subconscious fears or wishes from being allowed to impinge upon the results we obtain from our pendulum.

We want to gain real insights from our pendulum. This following exercise demonstrates an easy way you can practise remaining more impartial and also develop your ability as a dowser at the same time.

Take 6 post card sized pieces of card (post cards are obviously ideal for this!). In pencil draw on five of the pieces of card a circle. On the remaining card mark an X. Pencil is used because we will be turning them upside down and we don't want to be able to see what is drawn on the cards.

Through dowsing you will be finding the piece of card with the X marked on it!

On a flat surface turn the pieces of card blank side up. Then mix them thoroughly up. You need to have no idea where the X marked card is amongst the six possible choices.

Dowse over each card asking "is this where the X is?" until you get your YES response to find the right one.

You are fine honing your dowsing skills in this exercise, if you don't immediately find the X card this is only part of your learning process.

Repeat this exercise at least six times, mixing up the cards each time, and observe your number of successful attempts. This little exercise is invaluable in learning to trust your own dowsing and remain a little more detached from possible answers. The more you practise this, the higher percentage level of positive hits you will get.

ANSWERING THE UNANSWERABLE

We can all sometimes experience issues when remaining detached when asking questions of the pendulum. Thankfully, we are able to gain some unbiased clarity with this simple exercise.

You will need your pieces of card from earlier with YES, NO and MAYBE written on them. On a flat surface turn these three options blank side up, so you cannot read the writing.

The last time I personally used this method I found myself faced with a choice in life and knew I needed my dowsing responses to be uncluttered by my own thoughts and opinions on the matter.

Offered my own metaphysic centred radio show, I wanted to know if this would be useful way for me to inform others. My upturned three pieces of card before me, I dowsed over each one at a time, asking the question "should I accept this offer of a radio show?" to receive a positive response over the second card which turned out to be NO. And I duly turned down the offer, happy to trust my dowsing.

You can use the YES, NO and MAYBE cards whenever you want a pure dowsing answer.

Like for myself, it might even become a favoured method to get past your own emotional attachments and cut straight to the heart of the matter. And if your response turns out to not be what you thought you might have expected, then as with

Claire earlier, you can start asking yourself why that might be the case to then gain more insights.

Dowsing Lists

Dowsing of lists can be illuminating and oftentimes even shockingly eye-opening. The answers our pendulum gives cut straight to the point in ways we might have never consciously reached had we been logically procrastinating a decision.

If you struggle a little with bringing pictures into your mind when asking questions and keeping that image fixed there, dowsing from lists helps with focussing on one point at a time.

Pendulum dowsing allows you to be precise in making decisions and narrowing down options. Dowsing also makes it far easier to follow intuition and train ourselves to trust our instinctive feelings more.

For list dowsing you need a pencil and your pendulum. The pencil is held in the hand you don't write with, the pendulum in your usual hand.

The pencil is for pointing to individual items on the list. As you point to each item. hold our pendulum in the usual way and ask for YES, NO or MAYBE response as you progress down your list.

Below is an example of list dowsing to demonstrate how it is done. Here is a choice of possible holiday destination for my own winter city-break. Writing down six of the standout possible destinations gave me a list to dowse. Pointing in turn to each item to asking "is this the best destination for my winter city-break this year?"

POSSIBLE WINTER BREAK LIST

Manhattan

Toronto

Lisbon

Tokyo

London

Oslo

Once there is a definite answer the choice can narrowed down even further. Let's say Oslo indeed turned out to be the one city which got a YES response from the pendulum.

Wouldn't it now be useful for a little help in choosing exactly where to stay in the city? Having looked at a few options online next came a further written list. This time with options on where to book to stay in the city. Proceeding down the list in the same way as last time pointing with the pencil and asking "is the perfect place for me to stay during my winter city-break this year" Until a YES response is received.

Write a list for yourself to dowse. This can be about anything at all relevant to your life, and it doesn't matter how serious or trivial it may seem. The point is to give yourself at least six possible choices. Your list might relate to use my example on where to go on holiday or indeed anything else you choose - which lunchtime meal to eat; which book to read next; what shade to do your nails; which movie to see; which shirt to wear; where to move to a new house; who to invite to your birthday party or indeed anything you can think of that you can make a list out of.

Go down your list, pointing one by one to your potential choices with your pencil. Asking of your pendulum out loud or if you prefer in your head "is this the right choice for me at this time?". Until you receive your YES response.

Ley Lines and Investigating the Landscape

Alfred Watkins is credited with coming up with the term Ley Line and his wonderful 1927 book The Ley Hunter's Manual still makes for interesting reading. Born in the middle of the 1800's, Mr Watkins was a businessman and amateur archaeologist. He learned to be able to read the landscape; and through investigating firstly maps and then fieldwork, he noticed many significant ancient sites seemed to have been built across sometimes vast areas of the landscape in perfect alignment!

He coined the term Ley Lines to describe these alignments, through what he deduced were sites intentionally constructed to line-up along the earth's energy grid.

As we have learned more about the subject, since Mr Watkin's pioneering work, we now know Ley Lines are a network of energy lines which travel sometimes great distances through the landscape, often connecting significant ancient sites. The theory is that our Neolithic and perhaps even earlier ancestors knew of the earth's energy grid and planned their spiritual areas to be located along established Ley Lines. So forming a direct interconnection between themselves and their pagan deities.

Our distant ancestors were certainly familiar with earth energy.

Look past the surface of any ancient civilisation and it is easy to see evidence of their use and acknowledgment of earth energy lines.

Pyramids of Egypt and Mexico were constructed along specific alignments, Avebury Stone Circle is aligned at more or less the halfway point of a powerful Ley Line; and the ancient art of Feng Shui is centred upon the harmonious alignment of energy within the home and the greater landscape.

FINDING LEY LINES

It is possible to dowse for Ley Lines on-site. Getting out there into the landscape to follow hunches criss-crossing the land until your dowsing pendulum confirms the existence of a Ley

Line. Exhilarating as it is being right there dowsing while walking fields or hills; there is a far easier way to narrow down where Ley Lines are, and this is to firstly map dowse.

Ordnance Survey (OS) maps are ideal for our purposes. If you are searching for a well-known Ley Line, such as those linking famous ancient monuments, you can dowse over the map to confirm exactly the path of the energy for yourself.

Ask your pendulum for a YES response when you are holding it over the Ley Line, and by doing so, you will be able to mark in pencil on the map its exact path. And then if possible visit the location to confirm your dowsing with some on-site dowsing detective work!

If you want to discover some Ley Lines for yourself, perhaps from within your local area, again you will need an OS map. This time you will be dowsing grid references on the map.

Holding your pendulum go along the bottom of the map asking "is there a Ley Line in a grid-box above here?" until you have covered the entire area.

Assuming you get a YES response/s, next go down the left-side of the map asking "is there a Ley Line in a box to the right?". You can next dowse over the actual map, exactly where your pendulum indicated Ley Line to investigate further, which direction it might be going in and what ancient sites might it pass through.

There are positive energy lines (Ley Lines) and then there are also inharmonious ones, often causing Geopathic Stress.

GEOPATHIC STRESS

Kath and Leon found it difficult to sleep in their own home.

A new-build, they had lived there just under a year and something just didn't feel right from almost the first week. They both lacked energy, if there were any cold or flu viruses going around they both got them and more alarmingly they had the strong sense of unseen people walking right through their bungalow!

This is the one that kept them awake at night. Kath said it felt like people were walking through their bedroom wall, which looked out over the back garden, across their home and out the front wall of their lounge. Neither of them had been believers in ghosts, or indeed anything else unexplainable by science, and they were still inclined to want a rational explanation for their unusual situation. They didn't want to move on to a new house, just to feel at ease within their own home.

A little landscape investigation revealed around three hundred metres behind their house had once stood an ancient hillfort, the mound still visibly there indicating where it was. In their town there is a Norman Castle and on a large hill overlooking the entire town exists a bronze age burial site.

Dowsing showed a perfect alignment of these three sites and it passed right through the back-bedroom wall of Kath and Leon's bungalow, exiting out of the front lounge wall!

The strong negative emotion surrounding forts, their association with killing and war, plus the bronze age burial site that had once seen funeral processions walk the path from the hillfort behind their house, onwards to the hill, all proceeding straight through where their bungalow now stands and the Ley Line still carried all of this energy.

Fixing a small octagonal Feng Shui bagua mirror to the front and back of their property to deflect the energy cured the issue for them. They hadn't been sensing ghosts, rather powerful echoes of energy along the Ley Line; and after placing these bagua mirrors all unease vanished to allow them to enjoy their home and much increased positive health.

Geopathic Stress can result from a Ley Line of strong negative energy storing events of the past which are still being played out; or water passing deep underground below a property otherwise known as black streams and also pollution from background electro-magnetic energy.

If you feel you might have Geopathic Stress affecting your home affixing Feng Shui octagonal bagua mirrors to the outside of a property can deflect the energy; placing a crystal of Smokey Quartz near your front door helps absorb poor energy and electro-magnetic emissions; as can placing a few spider plants (Chlorophytum comosum) around the home.

Extreme cases of Geopathic Stress are, however, best left in the hands of experts on the subject.

UNCOVERING THE PAST

If you are interested in archaeology your dowsing pendulum gives you a key to unlock the past. It is simply a question of being sure to ask the right questions!

It doesn't matter if you are interested in finding lost burial sites in Egypt or an ancient Iron Age forge, dowsing can be applied to find any kind of long hidden archaeology. In cases like our lost burial site in Egypt when it is impossible to practically visit the site, map dowsing can be used in our detective work. In fact with any kind of landscape detection you do not need to leave the comfort of your favourite chair if you do not wish to.

This is for sure a handy method to narrow down potential sites, to later verify through field work when this is possible.

I have always possessed a keen interest in our ancient past and around three decades ago decided it would be fascinating to see if I could find out if there were any lost long-barrows in Derbyshire, England.

This is before the days of google, so I was happily able to dowse totally pure, with no pre-conceived idea if I would be successful in my quest.

A long-barrow is a Neolithic burial chamber, usually signified by an obvious hill standing out with in the landscape. Often down through the centuries through farming and other developments, however, these can get lost to view.

An Ordnance Survey (OS) Map of Derbyshire and my pendulum.

Dowsing across the bottom grid references I asked "is there a lost long-barrow located in an above square? To get my YES response.

Then going down the left-hand edge of the map asking "is there lost long-barrow located in a square right of here?. Gave me a positive YES.

By the way, this is the same principal that the ore and mineral dowsers use in exploration; it works in precisely the same way.

Having had my YES, I later set out on foot to explore within the area to see if my dowsing findings made sense within what I could see on-site within the landscape. Sure enough there were clear indications in a particular field I was exploring that a long time ago there could well have been something there, ploughed away through countless centuries of farming.

I was able to later confirm through some enquires with the Archaeology Officer in the County Surveyor's Office the existence of the long barrow.

With practice and the help of our pendulum, we can train ourselves to be able to live, at least a little as our ancient ancestors would have done.

Understanding our relationship to our beautiful planet and seeing the landscape as a living evolving entity, which we are all inter-connected with.

Learning to respect nature and her mysteries is all part of starting to feel through our intuition. Getting to the point where we can perhaps sense the energy in nature without actually needing to dowse at all, reading the landscape and trusting our inner knowledge.

What Do You Think?

We all listen to this constant stream of thoughts going on in our heads. Our own inner conversation with ourselves. We identify with this voice in our head as being the true "us" and naturally automatically tend to believe everything we tell ourselves through this constant inner chatter.

Yet how can we be sure though that every single one of these thoughts or inner conversations of ours is genuinely true? Most of us tend to believe everything we think all the time. Accepting it as concrete fact.

How about this one though?

When you were sixteen years old, assuming you are not sixteen now (and if you are sixteen "hi and kudos to you for reading this book!") did your set of belief patterns, what you were 100% sure life was really all about, match exactly with the way your belief patterns work right now?

You more than likely do not still view life in quite the same way you did at sixteen years old.

Although at the time, when you were sixteen, you were so sure your thoughts were correct beyond questioning them and believed them to be the absolute truth about who you are and the world around you.

OUR TRUTH EVOLVES

Dowsing can help a lot here.

How many times have you gone against some inner feeling of trepidation to nevertheless carry on right ahead with a course of action you kind of knew at some instinctive level did not sit quite comfortably with you? Like you I have also been there and done that. Haven't you found, as I have, that it seldom has a great outcome?

All too often these rationally worked out and procrastinated decisions can turn out to be those that are catastrophic in their outcomes.

We will do ourselves the biggest favour by instead developing a habit of trust in our intuition or gut instinct if you like. This bypasses all those egos driven conscious-level inner conversations we constantly have with ourselves and frees us to usually make the right choice.

Our imagination is one of the most powerful assets we possess. And has practically nothing whatsoever to do with logic or rational thought. It is instead listening to our intuition 100%.

In Tuition = learning to trust feelings and allowing our inner satellite navigation system to guide us through life.

Obviously not every decision we need to make will result in life-directional implications, yet why not turn to your pendulum to help with deciding where to go place that new house plant in your home, which winter jacket to buy or even what to eat for lunch?!

Dowsing ought to be fun and add to the quality of the adventure called life on this bluey-green planet of ours.

You can for sure bring your pendulum into play helping choose directions in life, enabling all the better to attune to intuition. Then at other end of the scale if you simply want to decide whether to have salad or a veggie pizza for lunch, then why not dowse and see what answers you might get? You have nothing to lose and you never know, you might well gain a lot.

The more dowsing is integrated into your daily routine the easier it will get and the more you will quite naturally find yourself trusting more your intuition.

In fact, as I see it dowsing as primarily for allowing us to develop a stronger connection to and learning to trust in intuition or what has been called gut feeling. The more you develop in your ability as a dowser, the stronger this becomes.

FACTS FROM FICTION

The cells of your body, the Universe works in a very literal way. What you think about creates your reality in every single sense.

Dowsing allows us to cut through any of our pre-conceived ideas when it comes to decision making.

Dowsing is invaluable in sorting fact from fiction, whether this originates from thoughts we are having or choices in life.

Dowsing And Meditation

Dowsing can act as a shortcut to intuition, creating the same kind of body, mind, soul connection meditators also nurture.

Yet meditation can also be a means to heighten your attuning to dowsing. Many decades ago when I first got into dowsing, I would always feel it worked most effectively straight after meditation. Keeping my pendulum by his side, after I finished my meditation I would then dowse for answers to any questions I had at the time.

Meditation can be relevant to people from all walks of life and all religious backgrounds.

Meditation certainly does not have to be a religious thing, for sure it is integrated as part of a religious practice, but it certainly doesn't need to be. It will be easily absorbed into most belief patterns as simply taking some contemplative down-time, to clear minds and move forward afterwards with less stress. As a stress relief meditation is invaluable!

DEAN FRASER'S METHOD OF MEDITATION

- You can sit cross-legged on the floor, as in the photo on page 45, or as you will have seen on the internet or television, the classic meditation posture or if you prefer to sit in an upright chair, that is fine.

- Hold your hands on your lap, with your fingertips and thumbs touching. Initially focus your eyes on an area of the ground about a metre in front of you, as you begin to concentrate on only your breathing.

- Without thinking too deeply about it, give your entire attention over to purely the function of breathing. Breathe deeply and slowly.

- Calming your thoughts as you start to relax. At some point you might like to naturally close your eyes. And continue focussing purely on your breathing.

- If any day to day thoughts attempt to intrude, re-apply your attention to breathing, count your breaths, one... two...three and so on.

- When you are counting your breaths, after a little while the outer reality of life will start to retreat, and you will find that you are deeply meditating!

- You can continue for as long as feels comfortable and to end simply open your eyes.

The answers we seek through dowsing, when no longer stressing about them, will invariably come via intuition and usually these are going to be the right choices for us to make.

Meditation is not a necessity to become a proficient dowser. The option to meditate is offered, as dowsing is principally about developing a stronger link to intuition, and meditation has the same goals. If meditation speaks to you and you wish to give it a go, keep your pendulum by you during the process and then when finished, turn to your pendulum to see if your dowsing insights are more profound. And, of course, if meditation isn't your thing, you can still become a highly skilled dowser through practise.

Signs to Take Action

The more you develop as a dowser, the more attuned you become to what is happening around you. By this I mean clues from the Universe that the time to act upon some of the answers we have received through dowsing has now arrived.

The term Universe describes the quantum forces of cause and effect that govern our life. Whilst synonymous with them, this term is not intended to replace deities or the god which are an integral part of anyone's belief pattern or system. It makes it simpler as dowsers to think in terms of the energy exchanges between our own pendulum and the greater world if described as Universe.

Universe represents love as a motive force, the power to transform reality in a moment. Just as we do when we seek answers to the unknown with our dowsing pendulum.

After a while, this interaction with the Universe when dowsing becomes as natural to you as opening your front door, you put your key in the lock and you are home. The same as when picking up your pendulum you expect to get the answers you seek.

Once you have been working for a while with the laws of the Universe or in other words consciously projecting your energy through being an active dowser, it becomes second nature to be aware of Ley Lines, and now you know that you have the potential to uncover the answers to untold mysteries, perhaps only limited by imagination. If anything can have an answer, then your pendulum awaits your questions.

Water

My Uncle Brian became a local hero back in 1976.

Here in the UK 1976 turned out to be the driest, warmest summer on record at that point. Wonderful for sun worshipers unable to get away to usually warmer climes for their summer holiday, but not quite so wonderful for farmers with scorched crops wilting and dying in the unrelenting drought.

Brian's crops on his small farm however seemed to be thriving, and naturally this did become a subject for village gossip. As Brian wasn't really one for socialising, eventually a neighbouring farmer could contain his curiosity no more and literally knocked on his front door to ask him how he managed to water his crops in such an extreme drought.

"Dowsing" Brian said. Nonplussed, his neighbour asked him to show what he meant. Brian took him down to the bore hole he had sunk in his nearest field, showed him the water pump bringing cool fresh water from three metres below the ground and explained he had found this water using dowsing. All scepticism gone, as the evidence before his eyes served as irreputable proof, his neighbour asked if Brian could dowse his land to find water for him as well.

Long story short – he ended up visiting many local farms that year in the quest for underground water. And up until ten years ago, when he finally passed away, his services remained in demand.

In the fourth book in this series I feel it is time to look more closely at water. After all, to many water and dowsing are inexorably linked.

WATER DOWSING TECHNIQUE

Brian was a rod dowser; he would walk the land until getting his YES response to the question "is there good water here?".

A pendulum can be equally as accurate, and indeed through map dowsing, we can narrow down geographical places to search before even heading out for field work. We need to first be sure when dowsing for water that we seek natural underground water sources. There was a farmer who prefers to remain anonymous, who took it upon himself to dowse his land for water. And having got a YES response, when he asked "is there underground water here" in a field quite close to his barn, then proceeded to dig up half his property in the quest for this hidden wellspring. Only to eventually realise his dowsing had picked up on some drainage pipes he himself had laid some ten years previously!

Dowsing can be very literal; it is up to us to ask the right questions...

When dowsing for water clearly the first thing you have to establish is "is there good water here?" and your pendulum will move in a YES, NO or MAYBE response to the question.

Let's assume you have a YES answer. It is quite useful to establish how much water there is underground. The usual way to do this is to ask "is there over 1000 litres? Over 2000 litres?" and so on until the answer is NO and then you know approximately how much water there is.

When dowsing finds water it can sometimes turn out to be many tens of thousands of litres, or even a natural spring buried deep underground.

So if you get to the point were seeking to know how much water there is and an obvious NO response doesn't come when questioning the quantity, chances are you have found a natural spring.

Whilst it wonderful and good finding some underground water, you will need to know if it can be accessed.

You might think that the next obvious question to ask then is "can we access this water?". And then oddly get a MAYBE response from your pendulum. Why? The pendulum has no idea if the water is easily accessible or not, as we failed to establish how deep down the water is or indeed how we intend to pump it up. Therefore the only possible response the pendulum can give to such a question is MAYBE. As always, the art is in knowing the right questions to ask.

You need to ask instead "how deep below the surface is the water, under 1 metre?" then continuing 1 metre increments at a time until you get a YES from your pendulum. Once you have established the depth of the water, then you need to work out which method works best to pump it to the surface. Brian used a small generator to dig a bore hole, then a water pump driven by the same generator to bring it to the surface and use.

If you have an understanding of engineering, you can ask which method will work best to access the water, or if you are dowsing for a farmer, chances are they will have the necessary skills to easily access the water you have found for them.

Water dowsing can also be useful for finding the mains water and outlet utility pipes to and from your own home. Especially helpful if contemplating any building or landscape gardening work.

If it is a nice still day walk outside with your pendulum asking for a YES response when over water pipes, which can then be marked out on the ground with pebbles or chalk. Windy days call for map dowsing. Draw a scale map of your garden and using the pencil pointing method, narrow down where the water pipes are; which you can then check later on site when on a calmer day.

Finding Lost Objects

The first time Lucy realised she had lost her wedding ring was when she came to drive her family back from their day out at Great Yarmouth, spending their time playing and relaxing on the beach. As soon as she placed her hands on the steering wheel she immediately went into a panic as she saw her ring was gone.

Together with her husband and three children they walked the beach where they had been, but to no avail. Yet Lucy oddly had an inner feeling that her ring would somehow be returned to her. Logically she knew her hunch made no sense, how could a ring lost somewhere on a beach, with no contact details on it, possibly find its way back to her finger?

She still felt it would do though.

The following day, when Lucy had a little quiet time, she took her pendulum and asked "is my wedding ring on Great Yarmouth beach?" strongly NO came back her emphatic response.

She asked "is my ring anywhere in Great Yarmouth?" again NO her response.

Suddenly she asked "Is my wedding ring in this house somewhere?" this question saw Lucy following her intuition, common sense would suggest no way could it be anywhere in the house. Clearly she had lost it on a yesterday whilst at the beach. YES came her answer this time!

She went through each room of her home, asking "is my ring in this room?" her entrance hall got a YES. Dowsing further narrowed down possibilities to the coat rack by the front door. All she knew that was hung there from the previous day was her backpack. Taking it down and emptying the contents onto a table revealed her wedding ring lodged inside her first-aid kit!

Thinking back she remembered she had delved into her backpack to retrieve a plaster for the grazed knee of her youngest daughter. Rather than emptying out her pack and risk getting it full of sand, Lucy had gone by feel to dig down into the full pack to grab the plaster out of her first aid kit; pulling her ring from her finger without realising it at the time. As an experienced dowser, intuition told Lucy she would find her ring, and thankfully her pendulum proved her right.

We can use dowsing to find any lost object, or at the very least discover where we actually lost it. If you are able to stay focussed on your lost object, then mentally retrace your steps asking "is my …… here?" (insert lost object). Until you get a YES response.

Narrow it down further, if physically possible by searching around the area further to ascertain the exact location. If bringing images to mind is more of a challenge, draw a rough map of the area you want to search. You can dowse over the map until you have found the location of your lost item; then if possible go to search, like Lucy did, and find the object.

Cleansing Your Pendulum

It is desirable occasionally to cleanse the energy of your pendulum. If it is made from any kind of crystal, gemstone, metal or wood, the easiest method is to pour only pure water over it for a few seconds. If you don't have mineral water or a natural spring handy, tap water will do as a substitute. Dry your pendulum with a natural cloth (cotton, hemp, etc,.) and then store it away in its pouch until next time it is needed.

Periodically cleansing our pendulum is a good habit to get into. Once a month or so is usually fine. Some keep their pendulum on a natural amethyst crystal cluster when not using it. This powerful crystal renders further cleansing unnecessary, the pendulum will be energised and cleansed purely from its time spent sat on the amethyst.

Putting It All Together

Dowsing is all about developing an inner link to our spiritual self and learning to trust intuition or gut instinct. Dowsing is not infallible and it certainly not an excuse to opt out of making decisions. Our pendulum shows us a possible course of action, the final decision is still ours to make if we decide to go with the answer or choose something else.

A dowsing pendulum is the perfect tool for guiding, nurturing our intuition and having the confidence to go with those choices which feel right deep inside.

Like with most things in life, the more you practise dowsing the more proficient you will become...

YOU BUT
STRESS-FREE!
DEAN FRASER

THRIVING!
A guide to making
the right choices
in life for you
DEAN FRASER

The Water Diviners

Treading the fields with his hazel twig
Showing farmers exactly where to dig
Parched crops wilting as far as eyes can see
Water hidden, over there, by the old yew tree
The water diviner struck liquid gold once again
A well sunk, the crops lifeblood soon to regain
Year after year, the farmer's gratitude enough
Brian the village legend always did his stuff
Is water divining passed on through generations?
There is one other, dowsing myriads of applications
Brian is his Uncle and yet his own path taken
Dowsing energy within the earth to awaken
Another time, another place, he explored his capability
His best-selling book enhanced his credibility
Having read his words, Uncle Brian nodded sagely
This wise man's approval mattered to him greatly
Two men, both of the Earth, doing their divining thing
Hazel twig, rods or pendulum in their hands swing
Two generations united in a common purpose, a goal
Helping others selflessly, find water, go dig a hole

Taken from Beyond Poetry by Dean Fraser